CONTENTS

First published in 1990 by
Kevin Mayhew Ltd, Buxhall,
Stowmarket, Suffolk IP14 3BW
E-mail: info@kevinmayhewltd.com

This edition © 2001 Kevin Mayhew Ltd.

ISBN 1 84003 810 1
Catalogue No. 1500459

Text: Stuart Thomas
Cover design: Jonathan Stroulger

Printed in Great Britain

PHOTOGRAPHS
Pictor International: Pages 2; 3 left; 3 top;
4 top; 4 right; 5 right; 6; 7; 13 left.

Robert Harding Picture Library: Pages 3
right; 5 top right; 13 right.

Tony Stone Images: Pages 5 left; 12.

Terence Burchell: Page 14.

ACKNOWLEDGEMENTS

The publishers would like to thank
The Reverend D. S. Meikle, St Matthews,
Ipswich, for his help in the preparation
of this booklet.

The marriage service from *Common Worship:
Pastoral Services* (Church House Publishing,
2000), extracts from which are reproduced
in this book, is copyright 'The Archbishops'
Council, 2000' and is reproduced by
permission.

Congratulations! You've taken the plunge and decided to become husband and wife. Your friends and family are probably celebrating the happy news and want the very best for you as you plan for the great day and start your life together. Everyone in the Church is pleased for you too, and will do everything they can to make sure the service goes really well. They want to make your wedding day one that you will remember for the rest of your life, not just for the joy and celebration, but most of all for the time you spent in church, making your vows to each other in God's loving presence.

Christian marriage isn't just about going to church and saying the right words. It's a lifelong commitment and needs to be taken very seriously, which is why a lot of prayer and thought will go into making sure you're prepared for it. This booklet is designed to help you as you get ready both for your wedding day and for married life. When you've read it, talk about the things which are most important to you with the minister who'll be preparing you for marriage.

THE COLLECT

God our Father, you have taught us through your Son that love is the fulfilling of the law. Grant to your servants that, loving one another, they may continue in your love until their lives end; through Jesus Christ our Lord. Amen.

FAIR SHARES

Apart from arriving in the world when we are born, and leaving it when we die, getting married is the most significant thing that ever happens to us. That's why newspapers record 'Births, Marriages and Deaths'. But unlike birth or death, marriage is something we can decide about for ourselves. So it really is the most important decision we can ever make. Have you stopped yet to think through why you've made that decision?

Whether you've known each other for years, or you've fallen in love at first sight, you know you love each other enough to want to spend the rest of your lives together. On your wedding day you express that love publicly, to emphasise both to the congregation and to yourselves how seriously you are taking this step. Later on, as your love deepens through the ups and downs of marriage, you'll realise how much that decision has affected your lives.

If you could think of only one word to sum up why you want to be married, you might as well choose 'sharing'. So let's take a look at what you'll be sharing.

SHARING A HOME

You'll certainly be sharing the same roof over your heads. It may not be a palace but it will be special to you as the first home you create. Living together as husband and wife, you're doing far more than organising suitable accommodation.

Home is the place where your love is centred. Your jobs may mean that you have to spend time away, but you'll look forward to coming home to share it with your spouse – even if the kitchen needs redecorating and the garden looks like a wildlife sanctuary! Home is where you feel secure, where you know you are truly loved, where you can be truly yourself. The home you create together will reflect your relationship and express something of it to those around you.

SHARING INTERESTS

Perhaps you've fallen in love through a particular interest you have in common – it may be working in the same place, or sharing a hobby or sport. This shared interest has brought you together and keeps you together. You've probably discovered too that you have similar values and attitudes to life.

When a couple first meet and start to recognise how much they mean to each other, they sometimes say, "We're just good friends", much to the amusement of those around them! It may be a cliché, but it's also an excellent basis for a sound marriage. But don't forget that a healthy marriage will also give partners both the space

and the opportunity to maintain and develop their own interests.

SHARING A BED

It's sometimes said to newly-weds that they shouldn't economise when buying a bed. A comfortable bed is certainly a good investment. However, 'bed' means sex as well as sleep, and you'll have various expectations about it, some of which may not be realistic.

A successful marriage doesn't depend on bedroom performance but sex is often a reliable barometer of how well a marriage is faring. Sometimes sex is called 'making love'. In a Christian marriage that is exactly what it should be.

Love-making may not always be physically 'successful', but if you're giving of yourselves to one another it will draw you closer together, enriching and deepening your relationship. Love-making binds together like nothing else can, healing the daily hurts and celebrating the joys of married life.

SHARING A FAMILY

More often than not families are the source of joy and encouragement, but at times they can also cause a great deal of irritation. You may need to be very firm about making sure that both your families are treated equally and fairly, otherwise resentment could start to take root.

This is particularly important if you have children – disagreements develop all too easily over how they should be brought up or what they should be allowed to do. It's also essential to set aside times as a couple to be quiet and private together, which should be respected even by close family members.

Children of your own will bring you a lot of happiness and reward, along with a fair quantity of annoyance and anxiety! You may not feel ready just yet for the responsibilities of bringing up a child and every couple feels apprehensive at the prospect of parenthood. But despite the upheaval

and chaos a baby brings with it, most new parents find the addition to their family a source of delight, and as children grow and develop each stage brings its own discoveries and pleasures. If you choose not to have children, you'll need to recognise why you've made that decision and how it affects your feelings. Some couples also have to face the sadness of being unable to have children.

SHARING FEELINGS

You can share a home, a bed and a family without having a particularly deep relationship. Some marriages function at that level. However, your love will only begin to deepen as you

share your feelings of love for each other – that's presumably why you've decided to become husband and wife! But there are still many things you've not said yet, either because there hasn't been the opportunity, or because you don't feel confident enough.

As your relationship grows and your love matures, you'll find it increasingly easy to share your innermost feelings. If you don't, your relationship could easily stop growing and become stale.

SHARING LOVE

Everything a husband and wife share is focused on their love for one another. A house becomes a home because the couple living in it love each other. Sex becomes love-making when it expresses their self-giving.

Children brought up in an environment of love, security and truth are more likely to become responsible and responsive adults.

Marriage without love is hardly a marriage at all, because love is the dimension which transforms all the other aspects of married life. It's that love which will see you through the hard times, enabling you to sustain one another and grow together as your relationship is enriched.

SHARING GOD

In choosing to be married in church you're expressing publicly that in some way you want God to be involved in your marriage: the Marriage Service expresses that not only in the vows, but also in the readings from the Bible, the prayers and the hymns.

God is love, and the love you share is a reflection of his limitless love. As you give love to one another you will start to open yourselves to receiving and experiencing God's love – that's why many Christians describe marriage as a sacrament.

In committing yourselves to one another you can discover something of God's self-sacrificing love as we see it in Jesus Christ.

It's perfectly possible to enjoy a successful marriage without making any Christian commitment. But by bringing God's loving presence into the very start of your married life you bring a whole new dimension to it.

That's the heart of a Christian marriage. God's presence day by day encourages and helps you; his acceptance and forgiveness of you enables you to accept and forgive one another; his love transforms your relationship; his strength sustains you through all the joys and sorrows which will come your way.

4 FIRST THINGS FIRST

Perhaps you are looking for the pages with all the useful information – like how to sort out the music and the flowers. Right now these issues are a high priority for you. But wait a minute. Your wedding day lasts for twenty-four hours – your marriage is for life.

What do you think you need to spend more time preparing for? The details of the big day are important, and you can have all the help you need to make sure the service goes well. But before that, sit down together and have a talk about these questions.

Q **What do you find most attractive in your partner? And what are his or her weaknesses?**

It's very important to be realistic about the love of your life! You'll be spending a lot of time together, and it's easy to take one another for granted. You need to say *what* you love about one another – and what you find irritating too.

Praise and encouragement make a big difference to any relationship – but beware of putting your partner on a pedestal, because it's very easy to fall off! Honesty about the things that annoy is also important, but you won't be able to change all of them – and shouldn't expect to.

Q **What things do you share an interest in, and what are your personal interests and tastes?**

We're all made differently. That's one of the joys of the way God has created us. Some people thrive in company, while others prefer a quieter life at home. Some enjoy a lot of excitement and action, while others prefer a more relaxed approach. Some are very emotional and wear their hearts on their sleeves, while others keep their feelings to themselves.

You may well find your partner is attractive because he or she is different from you, and complements your personality. But those differences can become a marital minefield if you don't work out how to adapt to each other and allow for them.

Q **How do you get on with each other's families? Can you see any difficulties arising once you're married?**

True, you won't be marrying your in-laws, but even at a distance some families can have a powerful influence. Do either of your families, especially parents, have a significant effect on the decisions you make together? Consider how this might affect your marriage, and how you might deal with it.

Q **Do you both share the same expectations about sex?**

A good sexual relationship takes time to develop, but you should start to explore your basic attitudes to it now. Some people come from families which readily express affection physically – others find it more difficult. Sex is the culmination of physical affection, not a 'marital right'. There'll be times when you don't much feel like having sexual intercourse, because of stress, anxiety or ill health but an affectionate hug will still do wonders for your relationship and speak volumes about your love for each other.

LYNDA AND MICHAEL'S STORY

Michael: *"When we married, Lynda had a good job and earned about the same as me. We each had our own bank accounts and shared all the bills. After the birth of Martin, our little boy, Lynda gave up work and decided to stay home until he started school. Quite soon we began to feel the pinch. At first, Lynda used to have her own savings for special expenses, but as her savings dwindled she began to get more and more irritable whenever we faced money questions."*

Lynda: *"Gradually, as my savings went down, I had to ask Michael for any money I needed. I had been used to being independent and I resented being in this position. Also, he seemed to think I was a spendthrift and not managing the housekeeping money properly. He never came shopping with me and never faced the fact of rising prices. Now Martin goes to playgroup and I have a part-time job, so we have agreed to share more in the running of the household. Michael sometimes gets the shopping these days and he is noticing prices more himself. But I wish we could have avoided those years of friction and money worries."*

What plans have you made to manage your money after you are married? Will you be able to live on only one income? How are you going to make sure that you've both got personal spending money each week?

Q Do you both want children?

You may not want to become parents yet, but some agreement on how many, and when, is essential before a baby arrives. You may also have to cope with an unexpected arrival!

Q How will you organise your finances and who will take responsibility for them?

Money is a major source of marital friction. The more open you are with each other, the less scope there is for suspicion and misunderstanding later. Do you have similar attitudes to money, and do you find it easy to agree about what to spend your money on?

Q If you both work, how will your careers and ambitions affect your marriage?

Will your working hours mean you see less of each other than you'd like? This may be one of the first issues you have to face – not many newly-weds can get by on one income.

Q What do you mean by 'lifelong commitment'? Are you willing to live by the promises you will be making?

We're all tempted to give up when the going gets a bit tough. Your promise is to stay together and be faithful, through thick and thin. Christian marriage doesn't have a trade-in option.

Q Why do you want a church wedding? Are you both happy with the idea or are you being pushed into it?

Of course you don't want to give offence, but neither should you let others make up your mind for you. If you're worried about this, talk to the priest who'll be conducting the service.

Q What difference do you think being married will make to you as people?

We all go through a constant process of change and development – usually the changes are small but over time they accumulate, and that's not always easy for the other partner to accept.

If you get into the habit now of talking to one another about your feelings and attitudes those changes will be a positive influence, and it's

much more likely that you'll grow together as a couple.

Q What else do you want to talk to your partner about before you get married?

Everyone has some anxieties and concerns, so don't pretend you haven't! You may even find you share some of them.

BE PREPARED

You may well be reading this booklet now because your priest or someone else at your church gave you a copy. (You may be married by a rector, a vicar, a curate, and she could well be female! In any event they're all priests, which is the term we'll use throughout.) They did so because they are responsible not just for the smooth running of your service and the legal arrangements, but also for making sure that you're ready to launch out into married life. They'll be willing to answer any practical questions or discuss further what you've been thinking through.

In the majority of parishes the priest prepares couples for marriage himself. However, there are some very large and busy churches which have a team from the local congregation to do this. Don't worry if this is true in your church – the people concerned will have been carefully trained to help you. In either case don't be afraid to ask about anything you're not sure of. Everyone will want you to be as well prepared as possible. By now the service will be looming large in your thoughts, so it's time to tackle a few practical details which you'll need to sort out.

● Before you approach your church about getting married there, it's worth finding a date which suits all those taking part, particularly if you have family members or friends who live abroad or who work unusual hours. In some places you'll also need to book the reception well in advance. However, you should bear in mind that your church will need as much notice as possible, especially if it is popular or pretty, as Saturdays can fill up very quickly.

● Your banns have to be called. If you both live in the parish where

you're getting married the banns need only to be called there. If either of you live elsewhere, the banns will need to be called in your home parish too, and you'll have to see the priest there to arrange this. If the banns can't be called for any reason, perhaps because one of you isn't a British citizen, you'll need to obtain a license – your priest will explain the procedure. (See the section on 'Marriage and the Law.') Don't forget that banns have to be called on three *consecutive* Sundays within three months of the wedding date – so leave enough time. If you regularly worship at a parish church outside your parish of residence, and would like to be married there, you'll need to be on the Electoral Roll of that church and have the banns called there too.

● 'Get Me to the Church on Time' is a song many priests would like some of their brides to learn! It may be a tradition for the bride to arrive late, but it is not a good one. If you're late it may well cause problems for those getting married after you, and it isn't good manners to keep your guests and the other participants waiting. When you book the cars, allow plenty of time for traffic delays (especially in busy towns) and any other unforeseen hitches. Check the arrangements for car parking. Many churches have limited parking facilities, and if they're on a main road it may not be easy to park outside. Many of your guests will be travelling by road and may not know the area, so don't forget to give them directions and some information on where they can leave their cars.

● As the guests arrive for the service they may enjoy hearing the bells ringing. If your church has bells, the ringers will have to be booked well beforehand, as they give their time voluntarily. A small charge is usually made for their services.

● A well-produced photo album will be a treasured memory of your wedding day, and the photographer will be one of the first people your guests are likely to meet when they arrive at the church. You should check in advance if your church has a policy about when and where the photos can be taken so that you can inform your photographer. Many churches permit sound or video recordings and will make some charge for this. A professional wedding photographer will be totally unobtrusive, but services are sometimes spoiled by an enthusiastic amateur who distracts everyone with a large flashgun and much rushing about. It's very much better to ask guests not to take photos during the service.

● A church beautifully decorated with flowers is an ideal setting for a marriage service. You'll need to check with the flower arrangers at your church how to organise this. Beautiful flower arrangements take time to prepare, and for this you may need access to the church on the previous day. If there are several weddings on one day, there may not be time to rearrange the flowers in between services. Ask about this well in advance to avoid disappointment and confusion.

● Music is a vital ingredient in the Marriage Service. It sets the atmosphere and enables everyone to join in singing the hymns. You'll need to book the organist and discuss with him your choice of music. The priest will probably suggest suitable hymns as he's responsible for all the music. If you have favourite hymns or pieces take advice before including them – some people might associate 'Jerusalem' with the Last Night of the Proms, for example. It's best to stick to hymns or tunes that most people will know, otherwise there will be an embarrassed silence. If your church has a choir they may be willing to participate, though you'll have to pay them the appropriate rate. If you have a relative or friend who's an organist, who you'd like to play at the service, you'll need to discuss this with your priest or organist at the church – the local organist always has the right to the fees.

Most couples have an order of service printed for their guests which contains the words of the hymns and responses. It makes an attractive souvenir of the occasion, but needs to be organised in good time. Check it through with your priest before getting it printed, otherwise you might discover an embarrassing mistake in the middle of the service!

Shortly before the day itself, you and the other main participants in the service will be asked to rehearse in the church. It's very important that you do this, so that you're completely familiar with everything that will happen. You'll feel a lot more confident if you've walked through it all beforehand.

You've probably chosen your bridesmaids, pages and best man. The priest may suggest you invite someone to read the lesson and even read some prayers. You'll need ushers, to show people to their seats, and also two witnesses to sign the register. One parent from each family, or the best man and chief bridesmaid are frequently asked to do this, but anyone can act as a witness if they are over 18. They don't have to be baptised or confirmed Anglicans.

If this sounds rather unromantically organised, it's better to make sure that everything is properly arranged in advance than to find your wedding day unromantically falling apart at the seams! If you're uncertain about anything don't be afraid to ask – far better to ask than let things go wrong. Different churches do vary slightly in their practices, but provided you co-operate with them, your Marriage Service should be truly memorable.

The service itself should be the central part of your wedding day, and it helps to remember that however much arranging you've had to do for the big day, it's only the start of your life together as husband and wife. It's easy to forget God in the planning. You're understandably preoccupied. So before the day itself give yourselves time to be quiet together. Try to read through the Marriage Service and think about what it means to you. That way you'll start to focus on God, on his love for you, the heart of Christian marriage.

MARRIAGE AND THE LAW

The laws of the Church on marriage reflect the law of the land. The words of the marriage rites have been worked out carefully between the civil and Church authorities, and cannot be altered.

a) Under civil law you may not be married until you are 16 years old. If you are not yet 18 you'll need the consent of your parents.

b) Most Church of England weddings take place after the banns have been called. You cannot be married in a parish where you are not a resident, unless you are on the Electoral Roll of that church. Banns must be called in both your parishes, if you live in different ones, and also in the church where you intend to be married.

c) Banns must be called within three months of your wedding day, on three consecutive Sundays.

d) If banns aren't called, you will need a licence in order to be married in church. A Common Licence is an alternative used where the banns have not been called. It is granted in the name of the diocesan bishop, and you'll have to live in the parish where you hope to get married (or be on its Electoral Roll) for at least fifteen days before your application. An Archbishop's Special Licence is used when neither of you satisfies the residence qualifications for banns, or if you want to be married in a building not licensed for marriages. You need the consent of the priest to obtain this, and the licence is *not* granted as an automatic right.

e) You may not be married if there is any impediment. In other words, you may not be married if you are still legally married to someone else, and you may not marry a close relative.

f) Civil Law insists that marriage takes place in an authorised place, before an authorised person, and in the presence of two witnesses. All parish churches and clergy are authorised by law. The registrar does not always need to be present.

g) The fees for a church wedding are standard. Your priest will explain what you have to pay and what that covers. You'll also be asked to pay the organist, choir, bell-ringers and anyone else who makes a specific contribution to the service. Many churches ask you to make a contribution to their funds to cover the cost of heating, cleaning and lighting.

THE MARRIAGE SERVICE

While for the Church the Marriage Service is an act of worship, that doesn't mean the social aspects are unimportant. The bride traditionally wears a beautiful white dress; the happy couple exchange rings and join hands; equally important, two families and sets of friends are gathered together. Marriage isn't just a private arrangement between two consenting adults – from now on society will recognise and treat them as a couple, so they make their vows in public to demonstrate that they're taking this seriously.

Of course, you could do all this without a religious ceremony, as many couples do. A Christian marriage service doesn't ignore the legal and social aspects, but it does place them in the context of worshipping God. So the solemn vows are made in his sight, and the rings blessed to symbolise his eternal love and presence with us. Above all, a Christian marriage service is a celebration of God's love, and an opportunity both to thank him for his gift of love and marriage, and to pray for the couple's new life, asking his blessing on their future together.

In the Old Testament God made a 'covenant' with the people of Israel, making their relationship mutually binding. Their commitment was to be loyal, faithful and obedient to him but they couldn't keep it up. So God established a new covenant with all people through Jesus Christ, enabling us to return to living in relationship with him.

By living in our world, Jesus entered fully into our life, sharing all our experiences of joy and sadness; in dying for us on the Cross, he brought us forgiveness for all the things we've done wrong; through his resurrection he opens up for us the way to eternal life. That's why the New Testament writers sometimes use marriage as a picture of the relationship between God and his people.

As you give yourselves to one another you can see a reflection of Jesus' utterly selfless love for us, giving up his own life to make that relationship possible. As you put your own personal interests to one side and seek the best for your partner, your own love and commitment will grow and deepen. At the same time, if your eyes are open, you'll see more of God's unconditional love for you.

There are five basic elements to any Christian marriage service – you may find it helpful to think of them as acts in a drama:

1) The entry of the bride with her father (or whoever is giving her away)
2) The Bible reading and sermon
3) The marriage vows
4) The prayers and blessing
5) The departure of the bride and groom.

Signing the register is a legal act, which in the new Common Worship Marriage Service is printed between 3 and 4, though it is also allowed at the end of the service; many priests prefer to include it directly after the couple have made their vows, though you may need to ask your priest about the practice at your church. Hymns are usually sung after 1 and before 4, with a third hymn before 5 if you wish, and even a fourth immediately before the vows. Again, consult your priest about the usual local practice.

An increasing number of couples request Holy Communion as part of their Marriage Service, though this is still relatively unusual. In mediaeval times it was normal for a couple, once they had made their vows, to go first to the Lord's Table to receive Communion before they went to their 'wedding breakfast'. After the Reformation this more or less died out, but the new service in particular allows for it. If you're regular worshippers you may want to mark one of the most important occasions in your life by remembering Jesus' death and resurrection and responding to his love for you. The service will probably take a little longer, but don't let that put you off! Discuss it in detail with your priest.

THE MARRIAGE SERVICE

For convenience the service described here is in contemporary language and taken from the new Common Worship services introduced at the end of 2000. Many couples are happier with this, but you may feel it's a bit lacking in poetry by comparison with the Book of Common Prayer. The differences are mostly in the style of language used, though at a couple of points there's a slight shift in emphasis. The Church of England doesn't regard either service as superior to the other, and you're entitled to say which you prefer; this too is something to discuss with your priest.

THE MARRIAGE VOWS

The high point of the Marriage Service, both for the couple at the centre of what's happening and for their families and friends in the congregation, will be the exchange of vows. The words may be very familiar but their importance can't be underestimated. So in the Common Worship service, as soon as the opening hymn has been sung and a prayer spoken by everyone, the priest reminds all present of the basis of Christian marriage, in the words of the Preface.

First, there's a reminder of *who* is involved in these vows – principally you, the couple who have come to make them, but also the congregation, who have gathered as witnesses of what you're promising. Marriage is too serious a matter to be treated casually or hidden away. What you're promising affects other people too, and from now on society will regard you as a family unit. Most important of all, God is present with you, and you'll make your vows to one another in his sight.

Second, there's a description of *what* the vows mean. God's relationship with those who love him is reflected in the mutual love of husband and wife. As they 'grow together in love and trust, they shall be united with one another in heart, body and mind, as Christ is united with his bride, the Church'. If we find this hard to understand fully, we can still accept it as God's gift to us, to be enjoyed, and treated responsibly.

Third, there's an explanation of *why* God has given us marriage:
• For the joy of having and caring for children – even if this is sometimes overtaken by the hassles! Children can be born of any male-female relationship, but Christianity teaches that they should be conceived, born and brought up in an environment of love, security and truth. Marriage provides that stable environment, and children whose parents have a secure, permanent relationship are better able to develop in a healthy way. The same holds true for children who are brought into a new marriage for whatever reason – stepchildren can benefit equally, find 'strength, companionship and comfort, and grow to maturity in love'.
• For sexual fulfilment – God created sex for our enjoyment and personal growth. Even if the Church sometimes seems to view it with suspicion, he certainly doesn't! Jesus taught that men and women were created for one lifelong sexual union, but

like every other part of marriage it needs to be worked at. Making love should be a 'delight', but because that's when we are most open and vulnerable too, we need the permanence and God-given security of marriage to really enjoy it as he intended.

• For mutual comfort and help – we weren't created by God for a solitary existence but to live in a relationship with others and enjoy their companionship. In marriage we can find our greatest fulfilment as people, two different but complementary personalities coming together to form a satisfying partnership.

The Preface ends with a restatement of how important the vows are. Marriage has tremendous scope for fun and laughter (some of your friends may follow tradition and try to play practical jokes on you!) but its implications are serious for all concerned, which is why at this point the priest asks the congregation, and you, the couple, to say if there's any legal reason why you shouldn't be getting married. The law exists to protect marriage and underline its importance to society. Banns have to be called or a special licence obtained before the ceremony can take place, which must happen between 8am and 6pm in an authorised place. These days you can't rush off secretly to a priest who'll marry you at the dead of night, so you now declare your legal eligibility to become husband and wife.

The priest says to the congregation:
'First, I am required to ask anyone present who knows a reason why these persons may not lawfully marry, to declare it now.'

The priest says to the couple:
'The vows you are about to take are to be made in the presence of God, who is judge of all and knows all the secrets of our hearts; therefore if either of you knows a reason why you may not lawfully marry, you must declare it now.'

It's very rare to hear of anyone objecting at this point to the marriage going ahead, so the priest now asks you to confirm that you're willing to proceed with the vows. The questions to which you will answer 'I will' date from a time when there was a public engagement ceremony. Everyone knows you've turned up at the church specifically to make those promises, but apart from confirming this according to an old tradition, you're also agreeing in public that your marriage will be based on Christian principles.

The priest says first to the bridegroom, then to the bride:
'N, will you take N to be your wife/husband? Will you love her/him, comfort her/him, honour and protect her/him, and, forsaking all others, be faithful to her/him as long as you both shall live?'

He/she answers:
'I will.'

A welcome addition to the new service is the priest's question to the congregation, who add their 'We will' to your 'I will's, emphasising that their role isn't simply as passive observers.

Just before those famous words are spoken comes the traditional custom of the bride's father giving her away (or another relative if this isn't possible or appropriate). It's not compulsory, and the new service doesn't include it in the main text, but Note 6 gives this option with a form of words. A more 'modern' alternative is also suggested, in which the priest asks both sets of parents (or other family members) if they 'will entrust their son and daughter to one another', to which they respond 'We will'. This latter emphasises that from now on parental responsibility has been replaced by mutual responsibility. Talk this through with your priest and agree how best to do it, if you wish to.

To conclude this part of the proceedings the priest invites everyone to keep silent for a moment before saying the Collect:

'God our Father, from the beginning you have blessed creation with abundant life. Pour out your blessings upon N and N, that they may be joined in mutual love and companionship, in holiness and commitment to each other. We ask this through our Lord Jesus Christ your Son, who is alive and reigns with you, in the unity of the Holy Spirit, one God, now and for ever. Amen.'

The service now moves on to the Bible Reading and the sermon.

Now, at last, we reach the heart of the matter, where you will make your vows to each other and then exchange rings. The service allows for a hymn to be sung before this, but many priests like to go straight on at this point.

The priest introduces the vows:
'N and N, I now invite you to join hands and make your vows, in the presence of God and his people.'

The bride and bridegroom face each other. The bridegroom takes the bride's right hand in his, and says:

'I, N, take you, N, to be my wife, to have and to hold from this day forward; for better, for worse, for richer, for poorer, in sickness and in health, to love and to cherish, till death us do part; according to God's holy law. In the presence of God I make this vow.'

They loose hands. The bride takes the bridegroom's right hand in hers, and says:
'I, N, take you, N, to be my husband, to have and to hold from this day forward, for better, for worse, for richer, for poorer, in sickness and in health, to love and to cherish, till death us do part; according to God's holy law. In the presence of God I make this vow.'

They loose hands.

It's not the Church that's marrying you – you're marrying one another, so to make the vows you turn to face each other. The practice of repeating the words phrase by phrase after the priest dates from the times when many people couldn't read, but it's still the most usual way.

Some couples like to read the words directly from a card, while others prefer to learn them by heart – it isn't particularly difficult and sounds well. But however you choose to say the words, you're accepting responsibility for each other as husband and wife, aware that life won't be all a bed of roses (even roses have plenty of thorns!). There will be times of illness, sadness, tension and anxiety to go with periods of joy, excitement and confidence. Your love will outlast all these and grow through them with God's help and in his strength. As you promise one another lifelong commitment and fidelity you know the only thing that can ever part you now is death.

The main text of Common Worship does not give the bride the option of obeying her bridegroom (nor does it give him the possibility of worshipping his bride). The word 'obey' only started to appear in marriage rites in the Middle Ages, and its apparently negative connotations today mean that increasingly few brides want to use it. However, if you wish to use it, you'll find it printed under the heading Alternative Vows, Form 1. It is also retained in the traditional language service which is still sometimes used, printed as Form 2 in the booklet.

The priest receives the ring(s) and says this prayer:
'Heavenly Father, by your blessing let these rings (this ring) be to N and N a symbol of unending love and faithfulness, to remind them of the vow and covenant which they have

made this day through Jesus Christ our Lord. Amen.'

The bridegroom places the ring on the fourth finger of the bride's left hand and, holding it there, says:

'N, I give you this ring as a sign of our marriage. With my body I honour you, all that I am I give to you, and all that I have I share with you, within the love of God, Father, Son and Holy Spirit.'

They loose hands and the bride places a ring on the fourth finger of the bridegroom's left hand, and, holding it there, says:

'N, I give you this ring as a sign of our marriage. With my body I honour you, all that I am I give to you, and all that I have I share with you, within the love of God, Father, Son and Holy Spirit.'

The relationship into which you've now formally entered is symbolised by the giving and receiving of rings. In the past only the bride received a ring, which is reflected in the traditional language service, but it is now common practice for both partners to give each other a ring, and Common Worship accepts this as the norm.

The priest first asks God's blessing on the rings, and as you then each place one on your partner's finger, you say the words of giving, which summarise what's been said earlier. You promise to engage in a full and lasting sexual relationship for as long as health allows; to withhold nothing of yourself within the partnership; and to provide for one another without stinting. The unbroken circle of the ring symbolises the permanence of your relationship, while the gold underlines your willingness to give of your all to each other for life. You do this in the name of God the Father, who created you as two unique human beings; God the Son who loved you enough to give his own life for you so that you can enjoy eternal life; and God the Holy Spirit, who will be present with you throughout your marriage. God cares about every part of your life and as you open yourselves up to him you'll be aware of his loving presence day by day, guiding and helping you and drawing you more and more into his eternal love.

'In the presence of God, and before this congregation, N and N have given their consent and made their marriage vows to each other. They have declared their marriage by the joining of hands and by the giving and receiving of rings. I therefore proclaim that they are husband and wife.'

At this point the priest joins your hands together and proclaims you to be man and wife, a relationship which is not to be altered. It is God's gift in creation, and no one has any right to damage or destroy it.

While the congregation remain standing, you as husband and wife now kneel before the priest to receive God's blessing on your marriage.

'Blessed are you, O Lord our God, for you have created joy and gladness, pleasure and delight, love, peace and fellowship. Pour out the abundance of your blessing upon N and N in their new life together. Let their love for each other be a seal upon their hearts and a crown upon their heads. Bless them in their work and in their companionship; awake and asleep, in joy and in sorrow, in life and in death. Finally, in your mercy, bring them to that banquet where your saints feast for ever in your heavenly home. We ask this through Jesus Christ your Son, our Lord, who lives and reigns with you and the Holy Spirit, one God, now and for ever. Amen.'

The priest says to the couple:
'God the Father, God the Son, God the Holy Spirit, bless, preserve and keep you; the Lord mercifully grant you the riches of his grace, that you may please him both in body and soul, and, living together in faith and love, may receive the blessings of eternal life. Amen.'

As you kneel and listen to the priest pronounce God's blessing on you, he will say a prayer asking for this to be not just in church, but also in work and companionship, awake or asleep, in joy and sorrow . . . even in life and death. There's no part of your future journey together from which God will be absent, and while there'll be times when that journey will seem very tough, the 'riches of his grace' are always available, without any strings attached, to help you and guide you through. As you enjoy the blessings of married life under his love, so you'll also begin to experience the blessing of eternal life.

The vows you've just made to each other before God now have to be ratified in law. Common Worship places the Registration of the Marriage directly after them, to underline that they are part of the same process, and to make it clear that the Church regards this as no less important. This is in line with what has become common practice. However, your priest may prefer for practical reasons to put this at the end of the service, which is allowed for in the Notes.

The choice of reading from the Bible is just as important as the hymns, and the service booklet gives a number of suggestions to help you make a choice, though you are not restricted to these. With your priest's agreement any suitable passage can be used. Probably the best-loved is Paul's famous description of Christian love and its characteristics in 1 Corinthians 13. His words apply to all human relationships, but they are particularly appropriate for the Marriage Service since they emphasise the quality of the love within a Christian marriage. Paul also wrote a letter to the Ephesians, from which two other suggested readings are taken. In chapter 3 (verse 14 to the end) we find a prayer that all who read it might know Christ in the depths of their being and realise the full extent of his love. In contrast, chapter 5 (verse 21 to the end) reminds marriage partners that they must love each other as Christ loves them and loves the Church, even to the extent of giving his life for them. Other passages you might wish to consider are Genesis 1 (verse 26 to the end) which tells how God created human beings, and 1 John 4 (verses 7 to 12) in which John also tells his readers about the nature of Christian love.

You may prefer to select a reading from one of the Gospels (you have to if you're including Holy Communion). In Matthew 7 (verses 21 and 24 to 27) Jesus' words stress the importance of building our lives and relationships on the proper foundation, while in John 15 (verses 9 to 12) he tells his disciples that only if they remain in his love will they be able to love one another with the same quality of love. The first eleven verses of John 2 contain a well-known account of Jesus attending a wedding himself – and adding greatly to everyone's enjoyment of the celebrations! It reminds us that he is present at every marriage where he's invited. Before you make a final decision, it's a good idea to read through several of the passages carefully. Even if you only use one, they'll help you understand a bit more about Christian marriage in the context of God's love. If you'd like something explained, your priest will be more than happy to help you.

THE MUSIC

A parish priest is responsible for all the worship in his church, including the music, and you'll have to check that what you've chosen is acceptable to him. In some churches there is a list of suitable hymns, anthems and organ music from which you are asked to make your selection; elsewhere you may be directed to talk to the organist or choirmaster himself, to find out what's possible. Inexpensive CDs of suitable wedding music are easily obtained in your local High Street, but it isn't good manners just to hand over a list of what you want. Bear in mind too that however competent they are, most church musicians aren't paid professionals, and therefore will only have limited time for practice. At the same time they'll have plenty of experience of which hymns and pieces work best – it's worth taking their advice.

THE PRAYERS

The prayers come near the end of the service, after you've made your vows, because they look forward to your life from now on as a married couple. Common Worship includes a wider range of prayers – for you as a couple in your life together, for the gift of children, for your families and your home. Some recognise sensitively that there may be a family already from a previous marriage or relationship, or that there may still be painful memories from the past. These aren't printed in the Common Worship booklet, but your priest will certainly show you the alternatives that are possible.

Most couples are content with these, but if your priest agrees you could choose some from another suitable source, or even write your own. The Lord's Prayer is included in every Marriage Service, and you'll need to decide whether you prefer it in the traditional or contemporary form. One of the loveliest of the prayers asks God to 'open your hearts to the riches of his grace', as you've opened your hearts to each other in love. In the same way that you enjoy each other's company, God wants you to love him and enjoy his presence too. His love within you will make all the difference to your lives and relationship, and help you live in a way which pleases him.

IF YOU'RE DIVORCED

The Church has always followed Jesus' teaching that marriage is a lifelong, permanent commitment to one partner. Sadly, the reality today for more than one couple in three is that their marriage will end in divorce. The process of ending a marriage is usually expensive and invariably painful, and most of those who go through it wish they hadn't had to. If you've been through the hurt and trauma of marital breakdown and divorce, the Church doesn't want to sit in judgement on you, or cause you more pain than you've endured already. Even so, some people have felt let down and unfairly treated by the Church when they've wanted to marry again after a divorce, so it's important to understand why your priest might hold a particular view.

Civil law allows a priest or minister of religion to conduct the marriage of any couple who are legally entitled to be married. However, the Canon Law of the Church of England doesn't yet permit this, which means in practice that you might encounter a variety of approaches. Some priests and congregations do not allow divorcees to be married again in their church, because they believe sincerely that to do so would go completely against their belief that marriage is a relationship which can never be dissolved. Others, while holding to Christian teaching about marriage, also want to emphasise that Jesus died for our failings and sins to be forgiven, and to give us a fresh start. So, provided both partners are sincerely committed to Christian marriage, they're

willing to consider marrying someone in church whose previous spouse is still alive.

Views are changing rapidly about this, and the House of Bishops has produced some guidelines which will shortly be presented to General Synod. Discussion in Diocesan Synods around the country has demonstrated a very widespread support for the principle of remarriage of divorcees, though with some reservations about how the guidelines might work in practice. It may be that by the time you read this section there will be greater consistency of approach between dioceses and parishes. However, there will still be a good number of priests who feel in all conscience that they cannot go along with this, and the guidelines will not force them into doing something against their will.

So if you're divorced and would like your second marriage to be in church, find out first what the local policy is. You may well find that your priest is willing, at least in principle, to conduct the marriage of a divorcee in church, and listens to your case sympathetically. You'll almost certainly be asked some important and searching questions, not to be intrusive in any way, but to ensure that you've thought carefully about what you're doing and intend to make this marriage truly Christian – many second marriages break down because the partners have made the same mistake over again. You'll be required to show your Decree Absolute, and to give assurances that any continuing commitments from your first marriage, such as maintenance and care of children,

are being honoured. You'll almost certainly be asked about when and how your new relationship formed, and your priest will also want to be sure that no public scandal will arise from you being married again. There may well be an expectation that you will be part of the local congregation too, so that proper pastoral care can be exercised.

However, if the answer is 'No', you shouldn't argue or try to force the issue – the reasons for the refusal will be genuine, and should be respected. 'Shopping around' for a priest who might say 'Yes' is also a bad idea. You might consider as an alternative the 'Service of Prayers and Dedication after a Civil Marriage', referred to often, though incorrectly, as the 'Marriage Blessing Service'. In a few places it's inevitably different from the Marriage Service, but it emphatically is not second best. Your worship of God and public commitment to each other are equally important. This service is included in Common Worship, and your priest will give you more details.

The debate on this issue will continue for some time yet but if you've been divorced, the Church will do all it can to help you – the days are mercifully long gone when divorcees were refused Holy Communion – and you'll find that everyone will do their utmost to make sure that whether you're married in church for a second time or have a Service of Prayers and Dedication, the occasion is truly memorable, full of God's presence, and a genuine fresh start.

WE DON'T TALK ANYMORE

Right now you're anticipating the biggest day of your life. It would be very surprising if you weren't anxious about how it's going to turn out – all the arrangements and planning are like so many pieces of a jigsaw needing to be fitted together. But you shouldn't have too many worries about your partner – if you have, you probably wouldn't be this close to getting married.

We've already seen how easy it is to forget that after your wedding day there's a whole lifetime of marriage. Even the most successful marriages couldn't claim uninterrupted bliss! You feel happy and excited now, and so you should. But just as there are no perfect human beings, neither are there any perfect marriages. Sooner or later you'll discover areas of tension in your relationship.

Perhaps you're both still 'on your best behaviour', trying not to offend or upset one another. That's very commendable, but it may also mean that later on some of the faults that aren't spotted now become rather visible. No-one can be at their best all the time – tiredness, anxiety and stress see to that. And as faults become more obvious, so it becomes harder to make allowances for them.

If you find your partner's behaviour driving you round the bend

occasionally, then it's vital that you say so at the time – get into the habit of sorting out your difficulties straight away. If you always say, "It doesn't really matter", you're stockpiling trouble for the future, and falling into the 'Green Shield Stamps' trap, storing up complaints until you've got enough to unleash in one massive argument. The golden rule is therefore – KEEP TALKING! If a conflict arises, deal with it there and then. Don't forget to praise and encourage your partner, though. You love this special person in your life enough to want to spend your life with him or her, and a little encouragement is worth its weight in gold. Most important, it helps you bring out the best in each other.

Both of you, without realising it, have received patterns of marriage and parenting from your own parents and families. You'll both have ideas, at times different, about who should do what, how and when once you are married. Even an apparently harmless situation can conceal an unexpected flashpoint.

However much you may think now that you can 'share everything' once you are husband and wife, in reality it won't quite work out like that. It's likely that for a while at least both of you will be working. Disputes can easily arise, for example, over which of two weary partners should cook the evening meal – or wash the dishes afterwards. Marital conflict seems to arise over such trivial issues, but all sorts of feelings lie beneath them – in this case maybe someone feels like a servant!

WORKING IT OUT

If you both have demanding jobs you'll come home feeling tired and stressed, and you may well find you're spending relatively little

time together. While you're both working you may have to accept that, but a wife who gives up her job or career to have children will soon become upset about an absentee father and husband. If your career demands more commitment of you than you give to your partner – beware! Infidelity covers far more than physical adultery; it's caused by anything that makes you give more of yourself than you do to your partner. Too many marriages are wrecked on the rocks of personal ambition.

TIME ON YOUR HANDS

A sometimes thorny patch of marital ground is how to spend your time. In a healthy marriage relationship both partners have their own interests and concerns, but difficulties will soon arise if one is always out practising sport or the other spends most weekends with their own family. You have to make allowances for each other's jobs, travelling time and rest – and don't forget that you'll both need time to spend with your families, to take a holiday and to relax together. If your job and leisure activities mean you see less of each other than you'd like, you may want to develop areas of common interest to compensate.

MONEY TROUBLES

Money problems are an all-too-frequent source of marital breakdown. You may prefer to keep your financial affairs separate, but that's not usually practical in the long term. Who pays the mortgage or rent? Whose salary covers the bills? Who buys the shopping? If one partner earns significantly more than the other, that can cause tension. Many couples find it better if just one of them keeps the accounts. If either or both of you are inclined to spend more than you ought, it's particularly important to keep a close eye on expenditure – and if you have credit cards, remember that they can get you into major financial problems before you realise it.

ALL IN THE FAMILY

Weddings are family occasions, and it's great for everyone to get together, perhaps for the first time in years. The love and support of your family are vital as you set out on married life. But you've now left your parents and 'cleaved to' your partner. That means that he or she is now your primary responsibility. Mothers-in-law have long been the butt of jokes, and most of them don't deserve it – but there's an element of truth all the same, and some families can cause serious difficulties, especially if they don't approve of their offspring's choice of partner. The parental instinct is powerful, and some parents find it extremely hard to let go of their children. Try to give both families an equal share of your time and attention if at all possible,

whatever your feelings towards them might be.

BEDTIME BLUES

Sex can set the flames of passion burning – in more senses than one! Nothing in marriage gives greater joy or deeper satisfaction than making love, but if sex isn't treated with respect nothing can cause more irritation and frustration.

You've probably got a good idea already of what you find attractive or unacceptable, and this will develop with your relationship. So it's vital to talk about sex openly and honestly – you'll soon overcome any sense of embarrassment, and find far more mutual satisfaction as a result. Unreasonable expectations of each other about sex will cause endless bedtime tension, so be considerate to your partner, and don't assume that he or she is feeling as passionate as you! On the other hand it's unwise and frankly selfish to withhold sex for any length of time or reason, apart from ill-health, and if you withhold it to manipulate or force your partner into doing something unwillingly you're not only causing unfair frustration – you're also breaking your marriage vows.

Much sexual tension can be dealt with by laughter, and a good sense of humour is a great asset in love-making, but if you feel your problems are more serious you should go to see your priest, a qualified counsellor, or a reputable sex therapist. There are other ways of demonstrating your love too – love-making isn't restricted to the bedroom or even to full intercourse.

THE PATTER OF TINY FEET

Sex leads on to the subject of children. You aren't obliged to have any, and in no sense do they 'justify' your union, but most couples look forward to the day when they will become three, four or even more. At the moment you probably don't feel remotely ready for the responsibility of bringing up children. Responsible family planning is available to everyone so you shouldn't feel pressurised by an

understandable parental desire for grandchildren, nor by some of your friends starting a family. Even so, it's worth talking about how you see your family in the future and trying to agree on how many children you'd like. It's not morbid but realistic to think how you'd cope if you couldn't have children, or had a handicapped child. Becoming a parent is arguably the most profound experience you'll ever have – and certainly the most life-changing! Despite the inevitable upheaval that follows, few couples regret having a family. Whenever you enter into parenthood, it's an experience that'll stay with you for life, and you'll want to give your children as happy and secure a home as you can.

When you become Mr. and Mrs., you become a family unit which is recognised by society and is part of a community. Even if you wanted to, you couldn't hide away in an exclusive relationship which locks everyone else out. You have family and friends, neighbours and work colleagues. As a married couple you can open up your home to them and welcome them – just as God welcomes you and wants you to enjoy his presence. If you only have eyes for one another, you won't see those around you, and you won't be able to focus on God. Marital conflict is inevitable, but provided that you recognise it and face the issues honestly together, your relationship will grow and be strengthened. Recognising them, talking about them, laughing at them, and taking them seriously (but not too seriously) will help you as you come to terms with a new life together – for better or for worse.

Q I was baptised as a baby but my fiancé wasn't. Neither of us is very religious. Can we be married in church?

A Legally you are entitled to get married in church whether or not you were baptised (or christened) as a baby. Some parishes expect at least one partner to have been baptised, but baptism and confirmation aren't part of a Christian obstacle course to be tackled and completed before you can have what you want!

Your priest's main concern will be that you're committed to a Christian marriage – so you should think carefully about why you want a church wedding. Is it because of tradition? Or perhaps because your parents and family prefer it? Maybe you want to do what you've seen your friends do. It may seem like the only way to mark such an important event in your life, but the Marriage Service isn't intended to add a romantic glow to your wedding day.

You're making serious promises in God's presence and receiving his blessing, so if you take it all too lightly the service will leave you cold. But if you're honestly seeking God's presence and help as you set out on married life together, your openness to him will make your service a very special occasion, one which will be a source of strength and encouragement throughout your marriage.

Perhaps you don't go to church because you've got too many other commitments, or because you had a poor impression of it earlier in your life. You've now reached a turning point in your life, and you may recognise for the first time that you need resources beyond your own. Whatever your reason for getting married in church, talk to your priest about it – he'll have helped many couples before you. You shouldn't feel pushed into doing something you're not sure about, but neither should you write it off. Take the opportunity to think about the Christian faith and

what Christian marriage means to you as you both face the future.

Q My fiancée isn't British. Are we allowed to marry in church?

A Yes, you are. If your fiancée isn't a resident in a parish here, the banns can't be called, so you'll need to get a special licence. Ask your priest to tell you how to go about this, and make sure you leave enough time.

Q Can we marry in my old school chapel?

A Provided the authorities agree and you have a clergyman to take the service, you can. Most school and college chapels aren't licensed for weddings, so you'll need an Archbishop's special licence. This involves getting the consent in writing of various people. The priest will tell you how to go about this, but again do leave yourselves enough time.

Q What happens if the banns aren't called?

A Banns have to be called in the appropriate parishes on three consecutive Sundays within three months of your wedding day. If you don't leave enough time, or someone forgets to read them, then the 'surrogate' (a local priest) will arrange for a common licence to be obtained. The cost is borne by whoever is responsible for the slip-up.

Q Does the Church of England object to contraceptives?

A Most couples prefer to settle into a pattern of married life before changing it by becoming parents. You probably need that time to get used to each other, and adapt to your new lifestyle. It's wise not to take on the responsibility for children until you feel ready. Various contraceptives are available, and there isn't any good reason why you shouldn't use them, other than your health.

It's vital that you discuss this

seriously, and come to some agreement about planning your family. A few couples decide for career reasons perhaps, they'd rather not have children. But don't assume that if you don't want a family now you never will. Many couples have unexpectedly found themselves on the way to parenthood, and despite initial doubts they've found it a profound and wonderful experience. It should be added that the Church strongly disapproves of abortion as a means of family planning.

Q We've lived together for three years. Why do we need to be prepared for marriage?

A You may know certain things about each other as well as some married couples. But you'll need a lifetime to know everything! At the moment the relationship is only temporary. Either of you can walk out at any time if things aren't going too well. On the other hand, marriage is a permanent and indissoluble relationship.You feel committed to each other right now, and that's probably why you want to be married. Marriage brings security and confidence to your relationship, and was created by God for that reason. You need to be prepared for the Marriage Service, of course, but take the opportunity to listen to what else your priest says, and look at your current relationship in that light. Getting married will undoubtedly enhance it, and if you're willing to listen and learn, could transform it.

Q Will the Church marry us if we've been living together?

A Yes, provided that you're legally entitled to marry. No-one will sit in judgement on you. The Church doesn't condone a sexual relationship outside marriage, but there are all sorts of social reasons why some couples set up home before they get married. If you're faithful and loyal to one another and are committed to a Christian marriage, God will bless you as he will anyone else who is open to his love.

Q My fiancée has just discovered she is pregnant. We were planning to get married next year. Can we still marry in church?

A Your fiancée's pregnancy doesn't prevent her from marrying in church. It isn't the best way to start married life, but if you love each other and want the best for your child, you'll obviously want it to grow up in a secure environment. There's no reason why your wedding day shouldn't be happy.

But do be sure that you want to get married. Baby or not, marriage is a lifelong commitment, and your decision should be on the basis that you want to make that commitment. Don't let others talk you into marrying if you don't feel it's right. It's better to remain unmarried than to go through the trauma of marital breakdown and divorce. Your baby's future is a vital consideration – divorce affects children every bit as much as their parents. Talk to your priest about it: but if you wouldn't have married anyway, think carefully before you decide to.

Q I want to marry a man who's been divorced for three years, can we be married in church?

A The Church of England has no agreed policy, so clergy will react to this differently. Some priests will say "yes", others will say "no". Read the section on remarriage for divorcees for more details, but in brief you'll need to show the decree of divorce, and be willing to answer questions about the previous marriage and any continuing responsibilities from it. Some priests won't marry divorcees under any circumstances, so there is the alternative Service of Dedication after a Civil Marriage.

Q My fiancée's brother is a Roman Catholic priest – could he take part in the Marriage Service?

A There's no reason why a Christian minister of another church should not be able to take some part in a Church of England Marriage Service. The priest whose church you'll be married in will normally expect to take some part in the service, and any other participants must be agreed with him. Some clergy from other traditions prefer not to take part in a service outside of their own. Clergy who are related to the couple being married often give the address, lead the intercessions, or do one of the readings.

Q Can we marry in my parents' home church? It's in an attractive village, and many of our friends live in that area?

A If you get married after the banns have been called, you must be resident in the parish where your marriage is to take place, or be on its Electoral Roll. Otherwise, you'll need a licence. You'll also need the agreement of the parish priests concerned. When you are married, you become part of the community in which you live as Mr. and Mrs. to be married elsewhere simply because of a prettier church turns the Marriage Service into a picture postcard affair, and trivialises the importance of the vows and God's blessing. If most of your family and friends are there, however, it may well be the most sensible option. Ask the priests concerned about this and they'll give you the advice you need.

Q My father is divorced, and was never baptised or confirmed. Can he be one of the witness?

A Any adult over the age of 18 can be a witness to your signatures on the register. Their marital status, religious background and nationality do not affect this.

Q I'm a practising Christian but my fiancé isn't. Does he need to attend church in order for us to be married in church?

A The Church doesn't force anyone to do something against their will. There's no barrier to you having a church wedding, so long as your fiancé is willing to accept the Marriage Service. You'll need to recognise the potential difficulties, however. You may find you don't always accept the same values and priorities. But you definitely shouldn't force your faith on him, or make a 'takeover bid'. He'll be impressed most by the Christian faith as he sees you live it every day – by loving him unconditionally as God loves us, you may in time make him realise your faith is worth sharing.

Q We've booked the Caribbean for our wedding ceremony. Can we have a Service of Dedication when we get back, or does it have to take place on the same day?

A An increasing number of couples are taking to the idea of combining their wedding ceremony and honeymoon in one, and a number of tour operators now offer very economical packages which deal with all the necessary legal formalities. If you choose to marry in some exotic location the ceremony may well have to be conducted by a local minister, though you should clarify all the arrangements before making a booking. However, if you choose to marry in England, in a building licenced for marriages, you should be aware that no license will be granted to any establishment with religious connections or decorations, and the ceremony must not contain anything even remotely religious, even a reading.

The Church of England doesn't disapprove of such alternative venues any more than it does of Registry Offices, but if you're concerned that your marriage be dedicated to God you may well find a purely secular ceremony rather cold and empty. As far as the Service of Dedication is concerned, it can take place at any time after the legal ceremony, and there's no reason why you shouldn't dedicate your marriage to God when you return home – in fact, there's every reason why you should! If for whatever reason you choose not to get married in church, no-one will hold it against you. Your priest will be happy to explain what the Service of Dedication involves, and should under no circumstances think of it as inferior – you're still dedicating your marriage to God and asking him to be present in it and give you his blessing and love.

Throughout this booklet we've been talking about Christian marriage. Clearly you have a Christian Marriage Service, and the vows you take express the Christian view and understanding of marriage over many centuries. But not all couples who get married in church would feel happy to be called 'committed Christians'. About half of all weddings take place in church, but only 5% of the population actually worship on a regular basis. So what is a 'Christian marriage'?

If you're practising Christians it will be important to you to share your faith and grow in it together. Many couples read the Bible and pray together, and find it a great source of strength and encouragement, though not all take to easily, and some don't really try to make it work. If you're both part of a church congregation, you'll find this, too, is a vital part of your relationship as it develops. But there's no set pattern for growing together as Christians, and it's very important that you don't attempt a takeover bid for each other's spiritual life, especially if you come from different backgrounds or traditions. As you get to know each other better, you'll find a pattern of prayer and worship that enables you both to draw closer to God and experience his love in your daily life, as individuals and as a couple.

If you wouldn't call yourself a 'practising Christian', you may feel worried about God being involved in your marriage. Perhaps you are not very sure what you mean by 'God', and the idea of going to church fills you with alarm. But don't write it off – you've invited God to be involved in your marriage by choosing to make your vows in his sight. If you're open to 'receive the riches of his grace' on such an important day, why not stay open to him on the ordinary days which will make up the best part of your future life? God's love and concern for you extends far beyond the big occasions. You might be surprised at the difference God can make to your life if you allow him to be the 'third party' in your marriage.

Whatever your past impressions of the Church, and whatever your worries about being a committed Christian, give God a chance. Initially that may mean going as an enquirer, not to join a club but to discover more about God. Don't be afraid to. You may well find others doing exactly the same. Of course you can enjoy a successful marriage without giving God a second thought. But it will be two-dimensional. As God is present in your life through his Holy Spirit, you'll discover that vital third dimension, and realise how your relationship can be enriched and transformed by God's presence into a three-way relationship.

CLARE & STEVE'S STORY

*"Long before we got married we had committed our lives to each other. Getting married was a way of making that commitment in public to those closest to us – our families and friends. Most important, it gave us the opportunity to 'give' our marriage to God. Knowing that marriage was **his** gift to us meant we could ask him to protect us and guide us in our life together, as well as making the vows to each other in his presence. As we now try to live out those promises we still 'share' our marriage with God, asking his help and guidance, and we believe our relationship is strengthened and enriched as a result."*

How are you going to practise your faith as a family? Have you talked together about praying and worshipping? Do you respect each other's views about this?

SARAH AND RICK'S STORY

"The Service of Dedication gave us what we thought we'd lost through Rick's divorce – the possibility of our marriage taking place in the presence of God and with his blessing. At first we weren't very receptive to the idea, but when we looked at the service we realised that it wasn't a substitute but a service in its own right. The service followed straight on from the civil ceremony, which was conducted very personally. But it was only during the service that we felt truly married in God's sight.

Although we couldn't exchange marriage vows, the service gave us the opportunity to reaffirm the vows we had made just before, aloud and in public, with both God and our friends as witnesses. Our initial disappointment vanished, and in our eyes we've both been 'married in church'."

Why is it important to you to have a church service? What difference will it make to your relationship?